WEIGHT LOSS SECRETS YOU NEED TO KNOW

97 Tips, Tricks & Shortcuts That Can Help You Lose Weight, Boost Your Energy & Live Longer (Even If You Have A Busy Schedule)

LINDA WESTWOOD

ventureink
P U B L I S H I N G

Disclaimer

This book provides wellness management information in an informative and educational manner only, with information that is general in nature and that is not specific to you, the reader. The contents of this book are intended to assist you and other readers in your personal wellness efforts. Consult your physician regarding the applicability of any information provided in this book to you.

Nothing in this book should be construed as personal advice or diagnosis, and must not be used in this manner. The information provided about conditions is general in nature. This information does not cover all possible uses, actions, precautions, side-effects, or interactions of medicines, or medical procedures. The information in this book should not be considered as complete and does not cover all diseases, ailments, physical conditions, or their treatment.

You should consult with your physician before beginning any exercise, weight loss, or health care program. This book should not be used in place of a call or visit to a competent health-care professional. You should consult a health care professional before adopting any of the suggestions in this book or before drawing inferences from it.

Any decision regarding treatment and medication for your condition should be made with the advice and consultation of a qualified health care professional. If you have, or suspect you have, a health-care problem, then you should immediately contact a qualified health care professional for treatment.

No Warranties: The author and publisher don't guarantee or warrant the quality, accuracy, completeness, timeliness, appropriateness or suitability of the information in this book, or of any product or services referenced in this book.

The information in this book is provided on an "as is" basis and the author and publisher make no representations or warranties of any kind with respect to this information. This book may contain inaccuracies, typographical errors, or other errors.

Table of Contents

Would you prefer to listen to my book, rather than read it?

Download the audiobook version for free!

If you go to the special link below and sign up to Audible as a new customer, you can get the audiobook version of my book completely free.

Go here to get your audiobook version for free:

TopFitnessAdvice.com/go/quick

Introduction

Weight loss should not equate with sacrifice and giving things up. Instead seeing it as an investment in yourself, an opportunity to expand your experience of food, and to enhance your experience of life will keep you right on track towards achieving your goals.

The weight loss tips presented in this guide are extreme because they are powerful, simple and so easy to implement that they'll amaze and astound you.

There are tips you can start straight away and ones you can develop and combine in tandem with other tips to optimize your weight loss program.

Be warned though, some of these tips are so extreme they'll make you angry.

Angry that you haven't heard of them before...

And most of them will save you money.

How does that sound?

A healthier, slimmer, and richer you.

What about happier?

Read on, you will be...

Protein Packs a Knockout Punch

A Metabolic Boost

To become the lean machine you want to be without having to be restrictive to yourself, think protein!

The importance of eating plenty of protein for your weight loss program cannot be overstated.

Studies show that adding the right protein to your diet helps boost your metabolism rate, meaning you will naturally burn 80-100 extra calories a day without doing anything else.

Obviously though, you will be doing more if you're serious about losing weight and that's where protein really comes into its own.

Helps You Stop Obsessing

Protein isn't just good for the body; it's absolutely brilliant for the mind as well!

High protein diets will actively restrain and suppress every dieter's biggest obstacle - obsessive thoughts about food!

Reports show that eating the right protein at the right time of day can diminish such obsessing by an astonishing 60%.

It combats the desire for late night snacking so will help ensure you don't slip up at the end of a day eating well.

The benefits of a higher metabolism combined with its psychological impact provide the perfect one-two knockout punch to eating habits that keep you fat.

Many Sources for Many Meals

Beef, chicken, pork and lamb are all well-known sources of protein but vary your consumption and include fish and seafood such as salmon, trout, shrimp and lobsters, and don't forget about protein rich eggs, beans and nuts.

Because protein is in so many types of food, you should easily be able to make sure you are eating some at every meal.

Forming this habit will work wonders for your weight loss program. You'll find references to many other protein sources throughout this guide so keep in mind protein's power and punch.

Plan What You Eat

Automate Your Eating Habits

Knowing what you will be eating will make a big difference to what you actually consume.

Planning your meals in advance will considerably reduce the likelihood of making a last-minute unhealthy food choice.

Think about the week ahead and decide in advance what you will be consuming, where and when, to help you hit your weight loss target.

Don't Skip Meals

Because Starving Actually Stores Fat

It is very important to eat regularly if you want to lose weight. Skipping meals isn't good and not only because you are more likely to binge later at night, but also because it can make the body go into fat-storing starvation mode.

As the body reacts to the periods of starvation it slows down the rate it burns calories meaning it can be harder for you to shift them.

Avoid this by eating well and eating regularly - mealtimes are important!

Complex Carbs Aren't Complicated

And Simple Certainly Aren't Best

Carbohydrates are simple, or complex.

Knowing the difference will have a massively positive impact on your weight loss endeavor.

Think of simple carbs as simple sugars. They are most commonly found in refined and processed foods such as breads, sugary sodas and candy.

When you eat these, your body quickly converts their simple sugar content into glucose, which more often than not, gets stored and turns to fat because you're not doing enough to burn them off.

Complex carbs though work differently and are far more slowly digested by the body. As an added bonus, they are often packed with far more nutrition and other health boosting properties to keep you on track towards your weight loss goal.

Fruits, vegetables and whole grain foods are great sources of complex carbohydrates.

And because they are often far lower in calories too - it's a real win-win for you and your body.

Simple Versus Complex - A Banana Versus Soda

Put simply, go complex to achieve the weight you want and see simple sugars as simply something to avoid.

Calorie for calorie, complex carbs are far more satisfying and they take longer to add up on your calorie count - eat a banana and you'll consume about 100 calories. Drink a can of soda and you'll add on 150 calories.

The soda will deliver sugar and sodium and be finished in a few gulps. It might taste like the real thing but it's really nothing in terms of giving you what you need and is a costly way to get your calories.

But the banana delivers far more in fewer calories - its vitamins, minerals and nutrients have their own benefits while the fruit's natural fiber will leave you feeling far fuller for longer than any soda.

They are super-convenient and (almost) as portable as a can of soda (when protected well enough against bruising) so you can have one anytime, anywhere and enjoy not just the taste but also the feeling and knowledge that each sweet, fresh, natural mouthful is doing you a world of good.

Hide the Frying Pan

Use Your Pots

If fried food is a feature of your diet, changing the way you prepare and cook your food will be a massive help in your mission to shed the excess pounds.

So, next time you automatically reach for the frying pan, stop! There's more than one way to cook your food and ditching the frying pan is a really easy and incredibly effective way to lose weight.

There are loads of ways to cook healthy food that will make you feel and look better, but using a frying pan isn't one of them.

Try roasting, grilling, poaching, baking, broiling, grilling, steaming or eat your food raw.

Just keep it out of the frying pan and watch the fat melt from your body!

Salad Surprise

Wrap It Up

Everyone knows eating salad is a great way to lose weight and everyone also knows a salad can be one of the most boring, least appetizing meals of all.

Well, it doesn't have to be.

If the thought of a plate full of healthy greens and garden vegetables immediately makes you yawn, it's time to start thinking differently and changing that plate to a whole-wheat pita or healthy tortilla wrap.

Pitas are perfect for stuffing, while wraps are wonderful for, well, wrapping all the fat-busting leaves, tomatoes, peppers and onions into.

Spice It Up

And salads don't have to taste as exciting as cardboard. You can spice them up with a few chili flakes or season with a splash of lemon to give your food a fresh citrus twist.

Tiny additions of delicious herbs and warming spices will transform your salad into something that may even excite you and will definitely help you achieve your aims.

Emergency Packs to Tackle Snack Attacks!

Be Prepared for Munchies and Cravings!

Sometimes you just need an energy boost. But too often we reach for a candy bar, a couple of cookies or bag of chips to revive us when we're lagging.

Proper eating will help reduce the occurrence of snack attacks but won't totally eliminate them. So being prepared will help you deal with the temptations to munch and graze when they arise.

Create emergency packs filled with healthy, tasty nuts, your favorite fruits or sliced and spiced vegetables to tackle the cravings head on.

You'll not only lose pounds, you might actually save money for the new clothes you're slimmed down body will need!

Win-win!

Red Pepper Flakes' Surprising Secret

Early Eating Means Less Chewing Later

One ingredient to definitely add to your shopping list is red pepper flakes

Eating them early in the day as part of your breakfast or with a midmorning (healthy!) snack has the amazing effect of reducing the amount of food you'll eat later on.

They help reduce your appetite and dramatically weaken the otherwise powerful afternoon cravings we're all tempted by.

Spray It on Don't Pour It Over

See the Difference Because You Won't Taste the Difference!

Investing in a couple of spray bottles could yield as big or even better returns for weight loss than investing in a pricey rowing machine

But like the rowing machine the spray bottles are not going to work if you don't use them.

Decant your dressings and oils into the spray bottle and use them when you are cooking and eating instead of pouring out the oil or dressing from the container.

You'll be amazed at how much further they go, how much longer they last, and how much money you'll save.

But most importantly you'll be thrilled at how much weight you are losing.

A spray or two of oil is more than enough to cover a pan, and a couple of blasts over a salad will spread the taste far further and use much less dressing than pouring or drizzling will.

You'll not notice any difference to your meal - if anything, using less oil will probably make the ingredients taste much better.

But you will soon begin to notice the difference the big reduction in the calorie count is making on you!

Applesauce Dips Are Divine

But Make Sure Yours Is Low-Sugar!

Applesauce is simply brilliant for helping transform a plain healthy snack into something divine and delicious.

Of course, avoid sugar-laden applesauce so as not to undo your best intentions, and use low-sugar applesauce as a dip to add an extra dimension to a regular banana or as an accompaniment with chunks of melon.

Protein for Satisfaction

It's Better Than Fats or Carbs

Up your protein intake and you'll notice you feel more satisfied after eating.

Try adding lean-protein with each meal and you'll body will thank you because it's far better for you, and more likely to leave you more satiated than either carbs or fats.

I hope that you are enjoying this book so far, and if you could spare 30 seconds, I would greatly appreciate you leaving a review on Amazon.com.

Micro-Warning

Think Before You Make It Go Ping!

What you put in your microwave you put in your mouth so make sure the food you're warming up or cooking is helping you lose weight.

Packaged pre-made frozen meals are super-convenient, especially for people leading hectic, busy lives.

But they are not always the best choice for someone determined to drop a dress size or get back into those favorite jeans.

If your lifestyle and its demands leave you little time for cooking and the microwave is your most used kitchen appliance, look closely at what you're cooking and warming.

Change from the unhealthy pre-packed foods to microwaving soy chicken patties, brown rice and steamer vegetables or veggie burgers.

The difference to your body shape and weight will leave you delighted!

Get Out of The Kitchen!

And Away from Temptation

The kitchen should be a reserved place for cooking and eating.

Try not to use it as a place for working or conducting other daily business, as you're far more likely to snack and eat more when you're surrounded by food and all its temptations.

Moving out of the kitchen will put a healthier distance between you and the refrigerator - you know the saying, 'out of sight, out of mind!'

Endamane Is the New Name in Snacking

Pods Packed with Nutrients

Endamane is a key ingredient and popular starter in many oriental restaurants and it should be adopted into your diet if you're serious about losing weight.

It's a fancy name for boiled green soybeans still in their pods. They're packed with fiber, protein, vitamins and essential minerals.

Just half-a-cup-a-day provides the same fiber as four slices of whole-wheat bread and the same amount of iron as a four-ounce chicken breast.

They're normally available on the frozen foods section and are a great, low-cost and rather trendy way to snack.

Salt

Cut It Out and Seriously Shape Up

Salt is a massive contributor to piling on the pounds and often one of the biggest reasons you are finding it so hard to slim down and shed the weight you want to.

Because salt makes food so tasty it's almost everywhere and many in the West eat twice the recommended amount daily.

It doesn't cause weight gain, it adds to bloating and can really hinder your efforts to lose weight.

It can also make you hungrier, thirstier and less inclined to make positive choices to satisfy such cravings.

There are some simple steps you can take to reduce your salt intake and maximize weight loss.

Checking for sodium content on food labels and putting back on the shelf those with high levels, choosing fresh food over packaged, and home cooked over restaurant meals will all contribute massively and positively.

Your puffy face and podgy belly will also quickly shape up just by cutting the extra salt from your diet.

And it doesn't mean having to endure mouthfuls of season-less, tasteless food. There are plenty of other alternatives to try

43

that will keep your taste buds buzzing and your meals appetizing.

Tip 16

Salute Soup!

It's Ping-Tasty-Tastic!

Soup isn't just filling, it can be extremely comforting, warming and tastily satisfying.

There are loads of recipes to make your own delicious broth and makes sure you make plenty when you do.

A big batch will leave plenty for you to keep for later. For extra convenience store the soup in portion-sized cups and that way you'll always have a handy, nutritious meal ready and waiting for you in the time it takes the microwave to ping!

Clean the Fridge

...And Your Pantry Too

When we say clean the fridge, we mean really clean the fridge out by dumping all that fatty-no-good junk food populating its shelves.

And when you've finished with the fridge it's time to tackle the rest of your pantry.

If it's too much to condemn all the food to the bin, share it out among friends and family - but be thoughtful for those, who like you, are determined to lose weight...you could, perhaps, show your generosity by inviting them for a healthy meal made from all your new ingredients.

Eating Out?

Find Out First What's on The Menu

The prospect of a special meal at a restaurant is like a potential minefield to any weight loss warrior.

Not only is it likely the chef only uses full fat everything, but it's likely you're going to be facing a full three-courses.

Even if you skip dessert you are still going to be left with the starter and main and given that appetizers are fried and accompanied by dips and sauces full of calories and fat.

If you can find out about the restaurant's menu - phone and ask or look on their website.

Knowing in advance what your choices are will make it far more likely to be the right choice in terms of helping you lose weight.

Swap Spreads

Taste and Waist

If you're fond of spreading a bit of cream cheese on your bagel or butter on your bread, swap to using peanut or almond butter and reduce fat and calories.

Try other, healthier spreads too and if you must have cream cheese or butter, make sure your choice is low fat and low-salt.

It won't have a big impact on the taste but it most definitely will on your waist.

Helping Your Significant Other

Make Their Lunchtime Fun

We are well aware of the modern-obesity epidemic and the need for people everywhere to lose weight or suffer the myriad medical and lifestyle consequences.

So, the chances are you're not alone in trying to lose some too - for whatever reason.

Given your significant other is probably eating the same food and living the same lifestyle as you, they too would most likely benefit by shedding a few pounds.

A fun way for you both to achieve this is by packing each other's lunchboxes - with healthy food of course!

Be imaginative and creative with your ingredients and not only will you both be surprised at what you'll be eating for lunch, the added motivation of helping each other will make a massive difference to your shared determination to achieve what you both want.

Including an occasional note or invitation to 'something, somewhere,' strategically placed in amongst the low-fat yoghurt and whole wheat wrap can help spice up a lunchtime - and what follows - no-end!

Eggs for Breakfast

Every Day's Different

Studies have shown that people who begin their days by having eggs for breakfast feel less hungry in the afternoon than those who ate a carb-heavy morning meal.

Eggs are so versatile too that every breakfast can be the same but very different!

You can go for Rocky-style raw one morning and just scramble the exact same mix the next for a totally different dining experience!

Meds the Way to Live Longer, Thinner

The Diet Not Tablets!

The Mediterranean diet is famously good for the benefits it provides the heart.

But studies have also found that it can help people lose more weight than low-fat diets.

Not only will you live longer, you'll enjoy your extra years experiencing life at the weight and shape you want to be!

A Good Night's Sleep Will Help You Lose Weight

Does Dieting Get Better Than This?

Researchers at Colombia University have found that better sleep leads to better weight loss.

Their study compared women who on average only get five hours sleep a night with women who manage to get seven hours sleep.

The results are startling - those achieving only five hours sleep a night are more than twice as likely to be obese as compared to the women who get seven.

Sleep deprivation is a cause of stress, and as you know, stress triggers the release of the fat storage hormone cortisol.

Levels of hormones associated with controlling hunger, leptin and ghrelin, are also believed to be affected by sleep deprivation.

Insufficient sleep will leave you feeling hungry, less satiated and with a stronger appetite - which combined with your tired and less alert mind will leave you weakened to temptation, fast food and unhealthy, fattening snacks.

The message is clear - aim to get a minimum seven hours sleep and you'll not only feel a whole lot better, you will release less cortisol and diminish your hunger.

Eat A Rainbow

Brighten Up Your Diet

Brighten your plate and lose weight simply by adding at least one brightly colored fruit or vegetable.

The more colors the better - a rainbow is possible if you plan your meals, and the wider the variety of fruit and vegetables you eat, the more likely you will achieve your weight loss goals.

No, toffee-apples definitely don't count, but where possible definitely do eat fruit and vegetable skins because that's where you'll find a bounty of anti-oxidants that will help you lose weight.

Wardrobe Matters

Lose the Weight and Keep It Lost

Reward yourself and help yourself stick to the new, slimmer you by making your wardrobe match up to your goals.

As you slim down, ditch those now-baggy jeans and donate your outsized clothes to really underline your determination to lose weight, and keep it lost!

M Is for Mustard

...And Saving 85 Calories!

Simply switching mustard for mayo in a sandwich will provide a new taste sensation and save an astonishing 85 calories.

Mmmmm! Marvelous!

Moisten Your Turkey

Make It Mouthwatering

Turkey meat is naturally lean and often saved just for special occasions like Thanksgiving in the US or for Christmas in Britain.

But it's also naturally dry, which may explain its infrequent inclusion at mealtime.

But it doesn't have to be. Make the most of its versatility by mixing finely chopped onions and a little olive oil to ground turkey to make mouthwatering - and healthy - turkey burgers.

Straighten Up

A Good Posture Burns More Calories

Improving your posture is an immediate, free and always available way to lose weight.

By simply straightening up you'll straightaway start strengthening your core and because you're working slightly harder to maintain good posture instead of a slump. You'll also add a small extra-calorie burn.

There's no excuse to put this one off until later - so do it now, straighten up!

Sleep Don't Eat

The Real Power of a Nap

Cravings can creep up on you when you're feeling tired and needing energy.

Rather than opening your mouth to swallow a sweet snack or some junk food, instead close your eyes and have a restorative power-nap.

You'll feel more alert and re-energized when you wake, and if you are still hungry, have a handful of nuts or some fruit.

Share It, Lose It

Get Support and Encouragement

Be open about your goals and the weight you want to lose and share these with your family and friends.

It's a positive life change and their support and encouragement will really help you keep focused on becoming the person you want to be.

Selfies Are for Losers...Of Weight

Document Your Transformation

Selfies are everywhere and you should be taking them too.

Taking a photo of yourself at least once every week will document your progress and show how your efforts at physical transformation are working.

Try and take the photo in the same place with the same lighting and make sure you get the whole of your body in the shot!

Once again, thank you for reading this book, and I hope you're getting a lot of valuable information. I would greatly appreciate it if you could take 30 seconds to leave me a review for this book on Amazon.com.

Careful with The Leftovers

Put Them Away Before You Eat

When you have dished out dinner, clean out the pots and pans of any extra food you have left over, and dish these out too.

Put these away before you sit down for your meal and that way, you'll save yourself from the temptations of seconds.

Remember, fewer mouthfuls equals more weight loss.

Drink It Up

...And Flush It Out

Resist a soda or sugar loaded soft drink and choose water instead.

Not only will you see and feel the weight dropping off you, adding extra water to your diet will help flush toxins from your body and assist with detox.

Tip 34

Look Out for Labels

...Or You'll Trade Sugar for Fat

"Fat free" and "zero trans-fat" labeled food may seem the most beneficial choice to make and lose weight but beware!

Your choice may not be quite as good for you as it's proudly proclaiming to be as foods labeled "fat free" or "zero trans-fat" are sometimes trading those nasties for extortionate levels of sugar or salt.

Look careful before you buy and make sure you're not simply trading one for something equally as detrimental to your mission.

Pause to Talk

Make Your Food Last

Enjoy your mealtimes and the company of others, and feel like you've eaten more simply by taking longer.

Gulping down your dinner can leave you unsatisfied and wanting more. Pause to talk and you'll feel fuller from giving your body more time to digest the food between mouthfuls.

Hungry or Thirsty?

Learn the Difference

This tip works to wash away the weight simply by making sure you're not thirsty rather than hungry.

We can mistake our body's wants and its call for something, so before starting to chew drink a glass of water instead and see if that's what you are actually craving.

The results can be incredible!

Get Your Oats!

Silence Afternoon Cravings

Make oats in the morning a habit and boost your ability to really stave off your afternoon hankerings.

Just a cup full at breakfast will set you up for the day's demands, with oats slow-release energy providing the fuel to get you through and help silence those afternoon cravings.

Ditch the Juice, Drink Milk!

Reduce Calorie Consumption

Studies show that overweight people who drank skimmed milk at breakfast consume fewer calories.

So, instead of drinking juice in the morning, try swapping it for a chilled glass of skimmed milk.

Not only will your body benefit from milk's natural goodness, you'll be avoiding the massive sugar content found in many apparently healthy fruit juices that considerably up your calorie intake.

Make Food the Focus

No More TV Dinners!

If you're eating, make that the subject of your focus. Distracted dining can undermine your best efforts; so, don't start chewing when you're sat down in front of the TV or in a movie theater.

Make food your focus and eat at set times, at a dining table (when possible) and you'll find you'll eat far less calories and therefore lose more weight.

Glycemic Index Isn't Complicated

Keep It Real and Keep It Whole Foods

The glycemic index relates to the speed by which your food affects your blood sugar levels and paying close attention to yours will help keep you properly energized and in better control of your appetite.

Foods are ranked on the index as either being high or low. Processed foods and candy are higher on the index than high fiber or protein rich rations.

The former is also far more likely to be over consumed given their packaging and non-specific portion sizes compared to a piece of fruit or vegetable. Whole foods like those and meat are far easier to proportion while processed candy, refined grains, juice drinks and chips all tend to be consumed in unhealthy quantities.

Learning to favor whole fresh foods rather than processed ones is the key to easily lowering your glycemic index and really optimizing your weight loss program.

A handy tip to remember if you are ever confused about what is or might be a processed food is to look at the ingredients in the product you are considering buying.

Processed foods normally have long lists of ingredients, often including several words nigh on impossible to pronounce for anyone with a chemistry degree. Avoid these and avoid foods with lots of E-numbers.

Keep it real and keep it whole when it comes to food to keep your weight loss on track.

Olive Oil

It's Brilliant but It's Still a Fat

It's one of the healthiest oils of all but olive oil is still a fat so use it sparingly.

Don't be deceived by its brilliance and use too much because it will undo your best efforts and add extra fat and calories to the healthiest of plates.

So, if you drizzle olive oil on your healthy salad, try mixing it first with some lemon juice to make a tasty vinaigrette with a far lower fat and calorie content.

CLA - A Secret Fat Burning Agent!

For Fat Loss and Muscle Gain

Ok, this one is a proper mouthful, which you may appreciate if all this reading is making you peckish!

CLA is Conjugated Linoleic Acid, a polyunsaturated, conjugated fatty acid that's found in many foods and as such is a natural part of the human diet.

It is primarily found in dairy products and meat and though a trans-fat (which comes with associated coronary heart disease risks) CLA is claimed to actually be a beneficial trans-fat.

You probably already consume CLA on a daily basis - and that's why it's worth bringing to your attention.

It is also available from health stores as a natural dietary supplement and CLA works to induce a combination of the holy alliance - fat loss and muscle gain!

Its benefits are believed to increase the metabolic rate so you naturally burn more calories and fat, whilst providing protection against fat gain after weight loss and thereby helping you to maintain your initial fat and weight loss in the long term.

Decreasing fat whilst promoting muscle growth is the key to becoming healthier and shapelier but the sad fact is that an astonishing 95% of people who lose weight eventually put it all back on.

That's worth chewing over.

Because the properties of CLA could be an extremely significant weapon against you becoming part of the 95%.

Research on CLA concluded that whilst it won't make big fat cells smaller, it does work to keep little fat cells from getting bigger which in turn makes you less likely to become fatter.

The hypothesis is that CLA assists glucose entry into muscle cells and thus helps prevent the glucose from being converted into fat.

Additionally, it is also thought to aid fats enter muscle membranes and connective tissue which are the bodies fat-furnaces where the bad is burned for fuel.

Chicken Dinners

Lose weight and feel even better when you save time and money by buying lean chicken breasts in bulk and cooking enough for the week ahead.

Chicken is a fantastic lean protein, great in sandwiches, wraps and with salads so try cooking a few extra breasts on a Sunday to leave you with plenty of healthy options for the working days ahead.

Eat Less and Live More

The Myriad Benefits of New Pursuits and Old Hobbies

Eating isn't only habit forming; it can be the only source of pleasure for some.

By taking up new pursuits or reconnecting with old hobbies such as music, sports, movies, concerts, walking, reading, etc., you'll find get new enjoyment and the added extra delight of losing more weight by consuming less and doing a little bit more.
You'll also feel more energized and far more sociable.

Apple Cider Vinegar

A Folk Remedy with Scientific Backing

Apple cider vinegar has been used for centuries for all kinds of household and cooking purposes - and now the properties of this ancient folk remedy are being utilized by many people wanting to lose weight.

All sorts of wondrous claims are made about the benefits of apple cider vinegar, and science has stepped in and validated more than a few of its fat fighting powers.

Consuming vinegar at the same time as eating a high-carb meal can really up your levels of food satisfaction and reduce the amount you eat throughout the rest of the day by between 200-300 calories.

Very handy then that it is a very popular ingredient in lots of condiments, dressings and vinaigrettes and some advocates even drink the stuff diluted with water.

Another study reported weight loss in obese individuals of between 2.6 and 3.7 pounds after 12 weeks consuming 15-30ml a day.

Vinegar is also known to reduce post-meal blood sugar spikes so you will reap the associated benefits of that in the long term too.

Speed Up with Spices

Chili Sauce Boosts Metabolism

Eating healthily doesn't have to mean eating plain.

Yes, if you want to lose weight you need to cut out the sweet fatty sauces, dips and marinades that liven up plain proteins such as eggs and chicken.

But swap those for a healthy (homemade!) chili pepper sauce or other spices and not only will you not miss those little calorie bombs, you'll actually speed up your metabolism meaning you'll burn fat and calories quicker.

Healthy Today, Great Tomorrow

Leftovers Make a Healthy Lunch

When cooking your healthy evening meal, make enough for your lunch the next day.

Add salad leaves, extra seasoning, spices or mustard to make it a little different and transform your leftovers into a wonderful wrap - whole wheat of course!

If you're enjoying this book and would love to let other potential readers know
how great it is, please take a few seconds to leave a review on Amazon.com.

Tip 48

Energy Boost

Optimize Your Exercise Time

By doing more and being more active you'll lose far more weight, but it's important to remember that your body needs nutrition and energy and that means eating the right foods.

Exercise can be off-putting enough without suffering an energy slump just after you've started working-out.

No problem!

Jazz up plain, low-fat Greek yoghurt and make it delicious by adding frozen berries.

Eat it before your gym session and it will charge up your batteries and give you a great energy boost to optimize the time you've set aside to achieve your goals.

Faster, Longer, Harder

Overcome the Plateau When Your Weight Loss Stalls

You've been eating well, exercising regularly and losing weight but then all of a sudden you reach a plateau and your weight loss stalls.

Don't be discouraged. It happens to most people and is a sign from your body that now you need to do a little bit more in order to lose more weight.

Adding an extra five minutes to your exercise routine will have you dropping the pounds again in no time.

A little extra effort also makes a lot of difference so you should aim to steadily increase your activity as you progress and become better and fitter.

If you haven't got the extra five minutes to spare, or if you're fitness class is only an hour long and will always be an hour long, work harder at the exercise, use your feet quicker, add an extra weight to the dumbbells, lengthen your stretches or shorten the breaks between using fitness machines.

Enjoying this book?

Check out my other best sellers!

Get your next book on sale here:

TopFitnessAdvice.com/go/books

Keep an Eye on The Clock

Avoid Munching After 7pm

Eating later gives your body less time to burn of those extra calories so you have to keep an eye on the clock if you want to become the weight and shape you've targeted.

Avoid late night snacks altogether and if possible, make sure you've eaten your evening meal before seven o-clock.

People who eat later are less likely to eat healthy food and also suffer a worse night sleep.

So, a good meal early in the evening will not only take you closer to your goals but will also improve your night's rest and leave you more energized, alert and awake in the morning.

Helping Your Significant Other

Make Their Lunchtime Fun

We are well aware of the modern-obesity epidemic and the need for people everywhere to lose weight or suffer the myriad medical and lifestyle consequences.

So, the chances are you're not alone in trying to lose some too - for whatever reason.

Given your significant other is probably eating the same food and living the same lifestyle as you, they too would most likely benefit by shedding a few pounds.

A fun way for you both to achieve this is by packing each other's lunchboxes - with healthy food of course!

Be imaginative and creative with your ingredients and not only will you both be surprised at what you'll be eating for lunch, the added motivation of helping each other will make a massive difference to your shared determination to achieve what you both want.

Including an occasional note or invitation to 'something, somewhere,' strategically placed in amongst the low-fat yoghurt and whole wheat wrap can help spice up a lunchtime - and what follows - no-end!

Apple Alternative

As Tantalizing and Tempting as Chips

The crunch and texture of a potato chip can be as tantalizingly tempting as the taste.

They are a keen favorite staple in many a lunchbox or as a satisfyingly convenient, tasty snack.

But yes, you know, eating them isn't going to help you lose weight.

The good news though is that you don't have to forgo the crunch and texture potato chips because apples can more than deliver.

Thinly slice and bake an apple, add some seasoning to taste (but go very light with the salt) and you'll have healthy, crunchy tasty chips that will work wonders with your weight loss program.

Feel Full

Water Rich Foods Really Work

We eat snacks for many reasons - a common one being because often we just don't feel full.

Between mealtimes we can feel empty and hungry and that is also when we are at our weakest to resist a vending machine's many temptations or store counter's treats.

Water rich foods such as melons, celery, oranges and tomatoes not only deliver essential vitamins and nutrients to the body; they also work to make us feel full up.

The water content works to leave us feeling more satiated between meals, working simultaneously to help us reduce the amount of calories we consume.

Step on Up

And Make You, Get You, To Where You Want to Be

Modern life makes living so easy - we are transported everywhere, often seated on our backsides or stood motionless yet moving.

To lose weight you need to become more active.

This doesn't mean having to join a gym or start doing triathlons, it just means noticing the opportunities around us to actually use our own bodies as a means of propulsion.

If you take the escalator at the mall use the steps. The same goes if you stand waiting for the elevator at work - use the stairs.

If you need the bathroom at home or at work, use the one furthest from you, the one on the floor above.

Take the stairs at the bus station, the airport, when you get the train or stay at a hotel.

These few extra steps and the little extra effort you make will burn more calories and also reacquaint you with your body's potential to get you to where you want to be - in more ways than one!

Have Your Burger Bites

But Hold the Mayo

If you want to lose weight but cannot bear the thought of life without a burger every once-in-a-while. You can still have your naughty little treat and eat it!

But instead of going for the super big-deluxe burger with all the extras and calorific trimmings, making a little sacrifice in terms of toppings won't deviate you too far from your righteous weight-loss path.

Holding the mayo, ditching the cheese and declining the top bun will effectively cut the burger's calorie count by a massive 250!

That's a whopping ten percent of the recommended daily allowance for an average adult male, and more for a woman.

Take A Break from The Plate

Think, Question and Honestly Evaluate

When eating your meal chew over the question: exactly how hungry are you really?

Do you really need to finish all of it now?

Taking a 30 second break from your plate to think, question and honestly evaluate the depth of your hunger may convince you you've eaten enough.

Fewer mouthfuls mean fewer calories so when you've thought about what you are eating, how much and if you have already actually had enough.

Make Your Own Dressings

Salad dressings come in all sorts of fancy shapes and sizes with eye-catching branding and promises of goodness.

The truth though is that what's inside that store-bought bottle or jar can be seriously overloaded with calories.

Mass-produced and made to maximize profit, salad dressings are often full of additives and extra ingredients to make them last longer and taste better.

By making your own dressings you'll know exactly what's going into them and how much better your own will work to help you accomplish your weight loss goals.

Buy a special bottle or jar - get a fancy one if you wish! And use it to store your own, homemade vinaigrette and dressings so you'll always have a tasty accompaniment to hand.

Thick and Creamy

Greek Yoghurt's Natural Texture Is Packed with Goodies

Thick and creamy does not have to be but a memory when you are determined to lose weight.

To achieve the same texture and feel on your tongue that warms up your other senses like thick and creamy magically does, use low-fat, unsweetened Greek yoghurt.

Highly versatile and loaded with protein, natural probiotics and calcium, the yoghurt makes a wonderful snack at any time as well as an extremely welcome, thick and creamy wonderfulness to many main meals as well.

Keep Your Co-Worker in Line

Make Your Own Snack Bowl

Your co-worker may not be the most sympathetic to your weight loss pursuit.

A bowl full of candy on their desk might be very funny to them because it will be frustratingly tempting to you.

Don't give them the satisfaction of seeing you give in and instead show your inner strength and resolve and make you own, delicious, exotic snack bowl.

Fill it up with small packaged portions of soy chips, baked apple slices, almonds and dried fruit and enjoy dipping in throughout the day and your co-worker's consternation.

Visualize Your Weight Loss

A Different Use for Sugar

You will lose weight from all your body so the difference at first and in the short term may not be so visible and apparent.

This can be discouraging and make you feel like work is not delivering good enough results.

Deal with these negative thoughts - next time you are shopping pick up a bag of sugar and allow yourself the time to really feel its weight in your hand and look at its size.

It probably weighs 2.2 pounds.

Holding and balancing the bag of sugar in your hands will help you appreciate how much weight and fat you have actually lost and give you the encouragement and motivation to carry on, do more and lose more weight.

And don't forget to put the sugar back on the shelf - if you're serious about losing weight you will be using healthier alternatives to satisfy your cravings for sweet things.

How to Measure?

Scales, Tapes and Old Pairs of Jeans

Scales are the first thing a person thinks about when thinking about measuring weight, and a tape measure's normally the second.

There are things to consider about which to use, given the peculiar nature of weight loss and how an inaccurate reflection of your body's transformation can be lost when reduced to statistics.

Scales will tell you how heavy you are, but if you are exercising as well as taking care about what you eat, be aware your whole body composition is changing - for the better!

You will burn off fat but will also add muscle. That's the goal and aim of virtually every weight loss program, but the also the key thing to remember when you step-up on the scales.

There's so much more going on inside you than a simple weight indicator can ever reveal so you need to consider other ways to really keep track of your progress.

A tape measure is great to record your vital statistics. Update this regularly to monitor your progress and really see the results you are achieving by measuring this way.

Another, far more personal method is to use your old clothes. Either the pair of jeans you want to fit back into; or comparing the end goal with the jeans you first wore at the start of your weight loss journey.

Simply trying them on every once in a while, and feeling how much looser the fabric feels on your skin, or how easier it is to get them zipped up, is a very motivational method employed by many pursuing weight loss.

Beat Your Meat!

Before You Slip It the Oven, Pound Your Portion

You can make your plate look fuller and meat portion far bigger if you give if a good pounding before cooking.

The act of tenderizing the meat with a pound spreads out the cut so healthy portions don't need to look like skimpy portions.

It's also a great way to relieve yourself of stress and helps burn a few more calories than simply slipping it in the oven does!

Nuts to Stop You Going Nuts

Almonds Are All It Takes

Clearly one of the keys to losing weight is beating that hungry feeling caused by just not feeling full enough.

That's when your weak and when the mind starts visualizing to the treats that start to make your mouth water.

It is an obstacle you can overcome by adding a handful of almonds to your daily diet to stop your belly's rumbles and your mind's loudening grumbles for those tempting treats.

They have the protein, fiber, and healthy fats, which your body is actually calling for and just a handful is all you need to stave off the hunger pangs.

They make a great snack if you want to eat them all at once, or you can add a few to a Greek yoghurt or mix in through a salad to instantly add texture, crunch and almonds distinct nutty flavor.

But remember to consume everything in moderation, because as almonds aren't low in calories, eating too many will undo all the goodness of chewing on just a few.

Grapefruit's the Great Fruit!

As A Tangy Waker-Upper

It is renowned amongst many people who have successfully lost weight - and for good reason.

Grapefruit is a low-energy density food. What that means is that a whole one contains only about 80 calories, has a decent amount of fiber and is full of satiating water to help you stay feeling fuller for longer.

It's high in vitamin C, contains vitamins A, E and B and plenty of minerals including calcium, magnesium, potassium, phosphorus and manganese.

It's a good source of essential oils and has loads of important nutrients.

And, its tangy taste at breakfast is a really great waker-upper in the morning!

Or for A Good Night's Sleep

What is less commonly known about the grapefruit is that it can be as good at night to help you sleep, as it is in the morning to wake you up.

Drinking (100%) grapefruit juice (with no added sugar!) before bed is believed to help prevent insomnia and promote a good night's healthy sleep.

Other benefits that underline grapefruit's status as The Great Fruit for weigh loss are its contributions to great looking, healthier, smoother skin, and not least its digestive work which can aid bowel movements and relieve constipation - some of the side effects associated when making a positive change towards consuming a good diet.

That Yoke Isn't Funny Anymore

Time to Drop It

It might look nice and bright on your plate and ooze its creamy-yellowness when broken, but ditch the yoke and you'll be ditching a whole load of extra calories too.

A medium egg contains around 70 calories - the yoke accounts for a whopping 50+ of these so you can see how eating only the whites will be far more beneficial to your weight loss pursuit.

Despite their low-calorie count, egg whites are still a great protein source - delivering 7 grams in only 15-20 calories.

Protein is for far more than just sustenance and body repair, especially for someone trying to lose weight because it works wonders on curbing an appetite and helps keep blood sugars level.

And because egg whites are so low in calories, you can indulge in a satisfyingly good-sized portion that will satiate you for longer.

Just be wise about how you cook them, and what you are eating with them!

Tip 66

Get Hormonal with It!

Chickpeas Make You Think

Neglected and overlooked by those not "in the know", chickpeas are a secret weapon in your fight to lose weight!

Eating the small, humble yet incredibly versatile and satisfying chickpea will release the hormone cholecystokinin and send signals to your brain that you're full.

As such, it's a powerful appetite suppressant and, because it's also a good source of fiber, the body will get the same message as the brain - you'll feel full and think it too.

You can introduce this legume easily and very differently to your diet in ways to make you wonder if it could possibly be the same thing.

You can toss them straight into a salad for ease, or turn your chickpeas into a tasty hummus dip and savor its creamy, crunchy texture.

They are also delicious when roasted and spiced with some metabolism-boosting chili flakes - perfect for snacking on or as a very healthy alternative to fatty-calorie soaked croutons.

Keep Your Metabolism Ticking Over

Too Few Calories Will Slow It Down

Radically cutting the amount of calories you consume will obviously help you lose weight but its effects are short term and extremely counterproductive.

Restricting yourself to consuming just 1,000 calories a day will actually slow your metabolism to the point where, in the long term, you'll struggle to lose any more weight.

What's worse is the fact that you'll actually start piling on the pounds as soon as you increase your calorie intake given your reduced metabolism won't be burning them off at its previous rate.

Definitely not a good idea as you won't just be feeling cranky and undernourished, you'll be frustrated and disillusioned by the return of the weight you fought so hard to shed.

It's important then, that your weight loss program isn't one that will leave you starved. Reduce the amount of calories you eat but do so in a way that will work best in supporting you to achieve your weight loss goals and to stay at that weight and shape once you have lost them.

Can the Corn Syrup

Cut It Out Completely

Science is showing a big difference between the effects of regular sugar and high-fructose corn syrups (HCFS) on weight gain and loss.

Lab studies have shown that drinking HCFS sweetened beverages significantly increases weight gain compared to sugar-sweetened drinks.

Studies are continuing but it's being speculated that the extra weight gain is down to the difference in the way the body processes each sweetener, with sugar requiring more work to separate the fructose and glucose.

HCFS is more easily and directly absorbed by the body because its fructose and glucose constituents are already separate.

It is important knowledge because of the prevalence of HCFS in many modern foodstuffs. It's in the soft drinks and soda we wash down our meals with, and can often be the primary ingredient in the food we chew.

Baked goods, desserts, many breakfast cereals, canned fruit and jams can contain large amounts of HCFS so pay close attention to the label of ingredients if you have to buy these.

Anyone who carries through on their pure intentions to lose weight will be giving these foods a miss anyway - but still make sure to check what you are eating to make sure you are not eating HCFS.

Tip 69

Breathe It in Before You Eat It Up

Science Shows the Power of Smelling

Giving your food a good deep sniff and really filling your nose up with its scent will help stop you filling your belly up too much.

Scientific studies have shown that just the smell of certain foods can help combat appetite and the feeling of hunger.

Grapefruit is an especially good food to smell when you're feeling hungry.

Chances are, you might still be feeling a bit peckish after a sniff and smell, but, yes, help is literally in hand as grapefruit makes the perfect snack to feast on given its high-water content, fiber levels and multitude of other health boosting-weight losing benefits.

Potatoes? Sweet!

Don't Dismiss These Super Spuds

Potatoes are in the starchy-carb category and are therefore shunned by many people trying to lose weight.

But don't allow yourself to be too hasty or dismissive of spuds because the delicious sweet potato can be a great ally in your battle against the bulge.

The average sweet potato is quite large in size but only boasts around 160 calories - which equates to only about 10% of a 1,600 calorie a day weight loss plan.

Baked in its skin, the average (5" long with a 2" diameter) sweet potato provides plenty of fiber at around 3.8 grams.

As the Academy of Nutrition and Dietetics reminds us, a high-fiber diet will help you lose weight because fiber curbs the appetite and thereby reduces the temptation and compulsion to overeat. It helps reduce blood sugar and insulin spikes ultimately helping to reduce belly (and other!) fat.

Put simply, sweet potatoes will leave you feeling fuller for longer on far fewer calories.

Perfect for Potato Salads

Make the most of sweet potatoes special taste and texture and transform some old classic dishes into modern favorites that will work with you to achieve your weight loss goals.

As always, be very careful when you cook them so as not to add calorie and fat laden oils and dressings.

They make an awesome alternative to regular potato chips - just slice then thinly and bake with some spices.

And if you're having a barbecue, swap regular white spuds for sweet potatoes to make a healthy potato salad (with a low-fat dressing).

Roasted and mashed sweet potatoes not only brighten up any dinner plate, they provide loads of flavor for very few calories.

They are highly versatile and can be used in all the ways regular potatoes are but remember, despite all their goodness, you will only optimize their benefits by treating them well - sinking them into the deep fat fryer for French fries unfortunately falls far out of this category!

Lean Bean Protein Machines

Brilliant Options

Beans are brilliant! Lean beans are packed with protein and a great, healthy alternative to meats.

They're wonderfully filling and very versatile, providing countless options for healthy main meals and snacks.

Others who are considering purchasing this book would love to know what you think. If you could spare a few seconds, they would greatly appreciate reading an honest review from you. Simply visit the book on Amazon.com.

It's Quality Not Quantity

Make Every Calorie Count Instead of Counting Every Calorie

If your weight loss plan is based around consuming a certain amount of calories, you'll already be familiar with counting the calorie content of each ingredient.

You know there's many, many ways to eat 1,600 calories a day, but you have to know too that in this case, some ways are most definitely better than others.

The secret is in knowing what else each ingredient is providing and think of it as a struggle between nutrients and calories.

Too often the concentration, the obsession, the focus and effort are on a specific number, and that is what catches many people out.

Your body needs nutrients, and more so if you are upping your other activities to really maximize your weight loss efforts.

Instead of counting every calorie you should instead focus on making every calorie count.

What to Look for And Why

Choose high fiber foods and increase the fullness feeling with extra satisfaction to suppress your cravings and reduce overall calorie intake.

Research shows eating an extra 14 grams of fiber a day contributes to a 10% cut in the amount of calories consumed.

Over the course of a week, this results in a 1lb loss in body weight.
And don't forget the importance of protein!

Research shows that calorie-for-calorie, protein provides far more satisfaction than fats or carbohydrates because lean protein curbs hunger pangs and cravings.

Focus on skinless chicken breasts, low-fat dairy foods, egg whites and super-lean meat to really shed the pounds.

Time to Re-Think Potato Chips

America Needs a New Number One

Potato chips have been the number-one snack food of choice for more than 50 years in the US. An astonishing 1.5 billion pounds of crispy fried spuds are crunched up and munched down every year in the States - that's an around four pounds each for every person!

Think how heavy a bag of sugar is and think how many bags of chips you'd need to balance a scale.

A few eaten occasionally what do you too much harm, but too many, too often can lead to all sorts of other problems related to being overweight.

It is claimed potato chips were 'invented' in 1853 so it's more than time to have a rethink - especially if they are your number one snack of choice.

Crispy, Tasty, Healthier Alternatives

There are loads of recipe ideas for you to make healthy alternatives to potato chips but such is their popularity that there's almost as equally as many options that you can buy from a store - and most of them come in the same kinds of rustly bags to give you very much the same dining experience.

Remember, they are still snack-foods so don't go overboard. You know by now that eating too much of anything isn't good for you; especially if you are trying to lose weight, so with these alternatives keep an eye on quantity, portion size and their preparation.

A bag of mixed veggie chips can have just a third of the fat and three-times as much fiber as their potato chip rivals.

For even more fiber, protein and less fat, try kale chips. They are air-crisped under low heat rather than deep-fried and are also an excellent source of vitamin A and loads of other nutrients and minerals.

Ancient Quinoa Is a Modern World Wonder!

Unique Complete Protein Source

It may be described a pseudo-cereal but there's nothing superficial, false or lying about the wonders of quinoa for someone intent on losing weight.

It's an ancient grain that has become a wonder in the modern world because it is unique in being the only grain that is a complete protein source.

Quinoa is the only one to provide all nine essential amino acids and leaves couscous standing in the race to deliver vitamins and minerals to your body.

It is naturally gluten free and particularly high in lysine - an amino acid that promotes healthy tissue growth and stimulates cell repair throughout the body.

On top of all that, it is a perfect accompaniment to many ingredients and can be served up in all sorts of ways to keep your palate surprised and make your mealtime delicious.

De-Stress and Control Cortisol

Relax and Cut Cravings

The fat-storage hormone, cortisol, is released by the body; this is the natural reaction to stress.

It's not a bad hormone and plays a very important role in human survival, but for a dieter and someone who wants to lose weight there's a few more things to know about how you can get it working for you instead of against you.

Cortisol activates sugar cravings, increases your appetite and can lead to general weight gain - extra fat around the belly isn't unusual among stressed out individuals.

Control your stress levels and control your cortisol production. Try some meditation techniques or breathing exercises to help you relax.

Exercise is one of the best ways to rid yourself of stress. And, yes, that's right, it's also one of the best ways to rid yourself of excess weight.

That's a real double whammy in your weight loss pursuit.

Don't Just Lose Weight, Burn the Fat

Take the Right Steps

Controlling your calorie intake in the right way will lead to weight loss. You might one day see the scales hit the right number but still feel dissatisfied with the look of the result.

It is a common experience but one you can avoid by literally taking the right steps to make sure you are burning fat and not just losing weight by losing muscle.

Research at Wake Forest University has shown that women who complement their calorie control with some exercise not only lose more weight, but burn far more fat from the important area around the belly and hips than those who just count calories instead of steps and gym reps.

Exercise not only consumes the calories you have consumed, but it really helps boost your metabolism, which as you know by now, really helps to burn fat.

So, if the look of your overall body shape is as important to you as your overall weight, the importance of exercise to achieve it must not be forgotten.

Wisdom of The Greeks

Half the Carbs and Sodium but Twice the Protein of Regular Yoghurt

If it taste's a bit too naughty it can't be nice and good for you, right? Well, in the case of Greek yoghurt that's definitely wrong.

It has a creamy, luxurious texture that you'd normally only ever associate with food that piles on the pounds.

But forget such received knowledge and think instead about Ancient Greek wisdom and culture - and how they also knew a thing or two about how to mix culture and milk.

Their yoghurt is heavily strained to rid it of liquid whey and lactose and create the tangy, creamy dairy delight.

Plain Greek yoghurt has half the carbs, half the sodium and more than twice as much protein as the regular variety. It makes a great alternative to other fats when cooking, especially cream.

But beware not to be too seduced too fast and check your choice is as healthy as it can be because some types of Greek yoghurt can be comparatively high in fat and lower in calcium than regular yoghurt.

Stand Up and Bear It!

Gravity Will Make You Lighter and Stronger

Research shows the body burns more fat and you lose more weight when your exercise includes more weight-bearing pursuits.

That doesn't mean strapping on loads of extra gym weights to your body - which will of course help you lose even more weight - but describes any activity you do on your feet and legs that works your muscles and bones against gravity.

You will burn more fat and also strengthen your frame and prowess by building and maintaining healthy bones.

Walking and running are the most obvious weight bearing exercises - but almost every team sport that involves chasing a ball is weight bearing so basketball, netball, and any other than keeps you on your feet will be great ways to start.

Dancing is another great weight-bearing exercise you can do when you socialize.

And for those still not quite sure, swimming and cycling are a couple of examples of non-weight bearing exercise.

Know Your Morph

Understanding Your Body Type Is Vital

Understanding your body type is important to fully maximize your weight loss efforts, especially if you are working hard and exercising while eating healthily. We are all very different but we all fall into one of three body types.

The first is ectomorphs and describes those naturally skinny types who have a fast fat-burning metabolism, are lightly muscled and appear to have minimal body fat.

Yes. If you're reading this, you're probably not an ectomorph.

But you might be a mesomorph (a lapsed one) as they are people with a natural, athletic build, good muscle definition and who can easily lose weight. If you are a lapsed mesomorph you will therefore find it easier to shed the pounds.

So, it's most likely you are an endomorph - someone with higher levels of body fat, who gains weight easily and has to work harder to shift it largely because their metabolism is sluggish and so works less like a furnace and more like a cold storage for fat.

If you know you're an endomorph you know then the likely benefits of what raising your metabolic rate will do.

Starving yourself and skipping meals is a definite no-no because that only slows down metabolism.

Eat foods that boost it and do exercises that will work to keep it ticking over at a higher rate between workouts.

A Is for Avocado

And as A Fruit Their Unique

Avocados are a unique type of fruit being high in healthy fats that have loads of nutritional benefits and potentials to harness for weigh loss programs.

The fruit is for far more than guacamole and prized the world over for more than its rich texture and meaty taste. It has become an increasingly popular choice made by health-conscious individuals and rightly wears its 'super food' label.

No wonder given it packs more than 20 different vitamins and minerals, and is a great source of energy, protein, fiber and healthy fats.

It's both cholesterol and sodium free, low in saturated fat and they contain more potassium than bananas - all worth considering when considering your heart.

The Long and Short of It

Avocados come in a variety of shapes, from pear to round, and its colors vary from green to black. They also come in various sizes and can weigh anything from 8 ounces to over 3 pounds!

By far the most popular variety is the Hass avocado, a.k.a. the alligator pear because of its skin texture and color.

Studies have found that people who regularly eat avocados are much healthier than those who don't.

Such people were far less likely to have metabolic syndrome, which describes a cluster of symptoms known to be a major factor in heart disease and diabetes.

Such people also weighed less.

They also had lower BMI (Body Mass Index) and significantly less belly fat.

Another study has shown that eating an avocado will leave you feeling 23% more satisfied and with a 28% lower desire to eat during the following five hours.

So, remember A is for Avocado so put them at the top of your next shopping list.

Keep Insulin Low to Burn Fat Instead of Storing It

Cut Sugars and Starchy Carbs Out

Dealing with cortisol is important but by far the biggest fat storage hormone in the body is insulin.

Consuming certain foods stimulates insulin secretion and therefore is to be avoided if you want to lose weight.

Cutting as much sugar from your diet as possible will really help, as well as avoiding starchy bad-carbs such as white bread, white rice and white pasta.

Lowering your insulin levels will release the fat easier from the body's stores of fat and with reduced carbs in the body, fat will become the fuel to power it so you will burn off far more.

And added benefit of lowering insulin levels is the effect on the kidneys' ability to shed excess sodium and water out of your body.

The result is less bloating and the elimination of unnecessary water weight.

It is not uncommon for people cutting right back on sugars and starchy carbs to find their reduced insulin levels leads to a weight loss of up to 10 pounds of body fat and water weight (and in some cases even more) after only one week eating this way.

You will have noticed too that sugars and starchy carbs are also the foods packed with calories, which anyone wanting to lose weight will avoid.

If you were hesitant about cutting sugars and starch before, you shouldn't be now.

Gum to The Rescue

It Works Both Ways!

Chewing provides all sorts of pleasure but it doesn't have to become a pain in your battle to lose weight.

Satisfy your need to masticate by chewing sugarless gum rather than a cream covered bun - it can also work to suppress your appetite to help you avoid the perils of snacking.

Take Control of Your Body Clock

As with almost everything in life, the older you get the harder it can be to lose weight.

As we age, we tend to lose muscle mass and correspondingly, depressingly, we increase our body fat.

In physically inactive people this process can start as young as 30, and for everyone it is associated with the basic fact of doing less and sitting down more, as we get older and more comfortable.

But unlike growing old, this is not necessarily inevitable and you don't you have to succumb to the effects of inactivity associated with aging.

Simply doing more will slow down this process, doing some extra and increasing your exercise will help prevent the loss of muscle mass.

Do enough and you will soon start building muscle and simultaneously burn more calories.

And because your muscles are growing your metabolism will increase so you'll burn even more fat and more calories making it easier all the time to lose weight, and then maintain a healthy weight.

And don't forget about shape and tone and how muscle is a sign of youth and vitality and essential in making the body firm, tight and shapely.

So get up, now, do something, burn off some calories, be active, burn fat, build muscle, increase your metabolism, burn more fat, more calories and so on towards a younger looking, more active, vital and shapely you.

Six Reasons You Can't Shift It

Understanding the Problem to Find Your Solution

It's a common, well know complaint: "I'm always dieting and I still can't lose any weight!"

It is also majorly frustrating and one of the biggest causes of lapsing or even giving up - what's the point when the results are so negligible?

Well, a little understanding of the problem will go a long way towards finding the solution and ending your dieting woe.

Honestly, It's Honesty

First, and most important is being honest with yourself and your body and actually appreciating how much you really are tucking away.

And that's not pointing the finger only at those who forget the little extras snacked upon throughout the day, it is also those of us who can't calculate for whatever reasons the actual amount of food consumed, believing it to be far less than is actually the case.

"It Is Just Not Acceptable"

Modern life and contemporary culture is such that nowadays it is almost unacceptable to be hungry.

We are surrounded by food to eat and blitzed by constant advertising telling us to snack on this or enjoy the mouth-watering finger licking new taste of a limited-edition burger.

But, actually, it's okay to feel hungry. It's actually healthy to feel hungry and it is a feeling you should allow yourself.

Misunderstandings, Backfirings

Misunderstanding how weight is maintained means you will also misunderstand how it's lost.

Drastically cutting your calorie intake or skipping meals are not sustainable or useful tactics to employ if you want to lose weight.

They may work in the short term but any benefits will soon backfire.

You will slow your body's metabolism and may actually prompt it to go into starvation mode, which means your body actually stores fat from calories rather than burning them.

You will feel less inclined to do anything and lack the necessary energy and nutrients to sustain exertion even if you try.

Modern Living Has Made Us Lazy

It is a plain fact that we are not as active as a species as once we were.

Technology and machines have freed us from the efforts of much physical activity, while transport of all kinds delivers us from A to B more often than we use our feet and legs to take us there.

It is a simple case of just not being active enough to burn the calories we consume. And it's as simple to fix by simply doing more.

Bigger Isn't Better

Bigger is believed to be better, especially when it comes to getting value for money and one way, we think we are getting good value is by getting bigger food portions.

Restaurants, especially fast food outlets and pizzerias that deliver or do takeout, have responded to this belief by making their burgers bigger, their fries more numerous, their soda cups wider and deeper and pizzas that now fill table tops never mind a belly.

It all means more fat, more calories and more likelihood of adding weight rather than losing it.

Be Social but Be Careful

So many social situations are now based around food that sometimes you just can't escape it.

You feel obliged to have the starter, and probably a glass of something to toast the occasion.

By the time you are ordering your main course your resolution may have already slipped so the extra cheese and cream or special crusted starchy carb becomes a "sure why not?" rather than remaining the definite no-go it once was in the not so long ago.

So, when the dessert menu arrives, yes of course you'll have a look and may be go for just a little bit of the pie and custard or chocolate cake with deep caramel sauce.

And as you finish the last mouthful you may even ponder whether or not you might get away with licking the plate!

Be strong and be committed to the promise you made to yourself of achieving a new healthier, lighter you and order wisely.

You know what you should eat so order it. And if you really aren't sure, ask the waiter for their suggestion about what's low fat, low calorie and still totally delicious.

Rinse Away the Fat Storage Hormone

Hydrate and Drop Your Cortisol Levels

Because cortisol is the number one fat-storage hormone, anything that works to reduce your cortisol levels and production will help you lose weight.

Dehydration is believed to be a contributory cause in raising cortisol and can be combated by drinking water.

Yes, the same zero calorie beverage you drink before meals to feel fuller and thereby eat less calories, works against cortisol.

So, drink up and drink often and help yourself hydrate to lose weight.

Flatulence and The Finer Points of Mastication

Chew This Over and Over and Over

Chewing your food is an incredibly important, effective and easy way to help you reach your weight loss target. It works in so many ways but is so seemingly minimal that so many people just don't fully exploit it as a weight loss strategy.

Like all the tips, this one isn't going to slim you down all on its own. But it will work wonderfully with others towards the delivery of a healthier, lesser you.

First, chewing is extremely effective against bloating. And it works against flatulence too.

You need to chew your food and masticate until you can no longer identify the ingredients by their texture.

It works because chewing is the alert for the digestive system to get ready to start its process. The stomach and intestines prepare to receive the food that chewing thoroughly breaks up into fine particles.

These are then broken down further and absorbed better by the gut. If you haven't chewed your food long enough or well enough it will only be partly digested.

This means you're not only missing out on some nutrients but also risking the consequences of undigested food being pounced on by the 'bad' bacteria in the colon.

This itself can lead to bacterial overgrowth, other symptoms of indigestion and, yes, flatulence.

Masticate your mouthfuls and give your weight loss chances a real and proper boost.

What's the Matter with Carbs?

Why White Is Not Alright

The type of carbs you eat, as you are learning, really matters and knowing the right ones to choose can really help you shed belly fat and excess weight.

Forget for now low-carbs and high-carbs and concentrate instead on the type of carbs you're eating - the effect can be massive.

The American Journal of Clinical Nutrition has published a study showing that people who ate whole grains such as brown rice, whole wheat bread, bulgur wheat and popcorn (the non-sweetened, non-butter glazed variety obviously!) lost twice as much fat from their midriffs as those eating exactly the same amount of calories but from refined grains such as white bread, white rice, white pastas.

Another report by Framingham Nutrition Studies found that women who ate 360 calories less than their peers still had more belly fat than women who ate the 360 extra calories because their food was far healthier with more protein, fiber and lower fat content.

It is believed that whole grains work so well by helping to keep levels of the fat-storage hormone insulin lower.

Lower insulin levels not only means less fat storage hormones, but it also seems to shrink the size of fat cells in the body.

Weekends Aren't a Break

Don't Be Seduced by Saturday Or Sunday

It's easy to get seduced by a Saturday and Sunday's leisure and rest time but remember, losing weight is a seven-day-a-week undertaking.

Slipping up at the weekend and 'allowing' yourself a little treat because you've been 'so good' during the week can really set you back.

Planning your exercise and diet for the week ahead can combat such moments of weakness.

It will remind you why you're denying yourself that cookie or bag of chips and motivate you to achieve your weight loss aim.

Think I, Apple

For Your Lifestyle

Before apples were the latest techno-gadget-must-haves, they were also a fruit. They still are and the natural green, red or yellow variety should be as much a part of your lifestyle as your iPad or iPhone.

Eating a fiber filled apple before a meal will really help cut your calorie intake because you'll feel fuller faster and eat less overall.

A Big Cheer for Chia!

Stay Strong

Of all the foods bestowed by the planet, chia seeds are right up there at the top in terms of nutrition.

They are absolutely packed with fiber and also contain omega-3 fatty acids, calcium, antioxidants, protein and 'good' carbs.

The unprocessed whole grain from South America has a naturally nutty taste that makes them a fantastic addition to foods and beverages.

Sprinkle them over cereal and yoghurts to extra crunch, taste and texture or add them in sauces and savory dishes and with other baked foods.

They have been consumed by various cultures for centuries as a great, sustainable energy source - 'chia' is an ancient Mayan word for strength.

But it's only relatively recently that they've become part of the world's 'superfood' group and are now consumed all over the planet for their health boosting benefits.

The high fiber in chia seeds promotes that satisfied feeling of fullness for longer which results in less overall snacking and by consequence calories.

Fiber also helps with digestion as an aid to the healthy bacteria in the intestine.

The humble chia seed is 40% fiber by weight making them one of the world's ultimate fiber sources.

And, as an excellent provider of protein and amino acids, they really help tackle cravings and appetite and can help significantly reduce the temptations that arrive late at night for a nibble and snack - a huge advantage for people trying to lose weight.

When consumed, the fiber in chia seeds starts to absorb water and thereby expand in the belly. That works to increase feelings of fullness and decrease the rate of food absorption. The protein works to help suppress your appetite.

While studies have not yet shown chia seeds to have an impact on weight loss by themselves, their remarkable nutritional content has persuaded many health-conscious people and others who want to become healthier, introduce them to their diets and combine them with other good, healthy foods to achieve their body weight and shape goals.

Pasta Less for More Weight Loss

Zucchini Magic

Pasta is packed with carbs and though brown pasta is actually quite healthy, it is still too calorie-packed for some.

Help is at hand though for spaghetti lovers and comes in the form of the highly versatile zucchini.

Adding veggie or lean meatballs, raw tomato sauce and some zesty oregano to shredded zucchini makes a pasta-less yet spaghetti style tasty treat that any Italian would be proud of.

I hope you have learned something from this book so far and would greatly appreciate it if you could leave an honest review on Amazon.com.

Savor the Smell, Taste, Touch, Look and Sound of Your Food

Maximize Sensual Pleasure to Maximize Weight Loss

Paying attention to the sensual delight of eating food can really help you lose weight in many ways.

It's a sensory experience to be savored and by doing so you will boost enormously your levels of satisfaction derived from what you eat.

Taste your food with your eyes, ears and nose as much as on your tongue. Look at its color, feel its freshness and texture open up the delicious flavors and seasonings.

It will leave you satisfied far more than if you just wolf it down when you're preoccupied with what's on the TV or the desk in front of you.

Maximizing the pleasure of each plate, each mouthful will help you reduce your portion sizes and by virtue total calorie intake.

You simply won't need to munch as much because, as scientists say, healthy eating is as much about the brain as the body (especially the belly!)

Lift Weights to Drop Your Own Weight

Anywhere, Anytime - No Need for Expensive Gym Memberships

You don't need an expensive membership at a fancy gym to lift weights - look at yourself and remember the benefits of weight bearing.

Push-ups, squats, sit-ups and belly crunches will all help you attain your weight loss goal and can be done virtually anywhere at any time, depending on how eccentric you are!

For those more introverted and less inclined to do ten push-ups in public, you can of course do them in the privacy of your own home.

A couple of minutes effort a few times throughout the day will have an enormous difference to your body shape and overall weight because weight lifting, including lifting your own weight, is pretty much the only proven strategy to keep your metabolism ticking over at a calorie and fat burning rate when you reduce calorie intake.

Put simply, you will burn fat instead of losing muscle and end up looking and feeling far stronger, healthier and far happier with the weight you achieve.

It's comparatively very little effort for a whole plentitude of benefits.

The Way to A More Elegant, Shapely Healthier You

As with protein, so with weight lifting - its importance cannot be overstated if you want to achieve, and vitally, maintain your weight loss in a healthy, beneficial way.

Weight training reduces your risk of picking up other injuries by increasing your strength. It improves bone density and can dramatically help improve your posture to make you look more graceful and elegant.

It works to tone and smooth your body so you'll look younger and more vibrant, better on the beach and out and about as your clothes will fit better and be far more flattering as a result.

And that's without considering all the other benefits associated with introducing some weight training into your life such as improved insulin resistance, blood pressure and digestion, and reduced risks of heart disease, cancer and diabetes.

Muscle and Fat

It's an old saying that when you stop weight training your muscle turns to fat. And like many other old sayings, modern science proves it to be totally untrue.

That's because of the simple reason that muscle and fat are two completely different types of body tissue.

One cannot become the other and so the other old saying that exercise turns fat into muscle is as equally nonsense.

Bad food and inactivity will cause you to lose muscle and replace that with fat.

And vice-versa - a eating good food and becoming more active will cause you to build muscle and burn fat.

There's no mystical, biological alchemy occurring to magically transform one into the other, no matter what impression old sayings may leave.

Apps for Counting Calories

They Keep Track to Keep You on Track

Calorie counting works for achieving weight loss. Some derive more pleasure and benefits than others from adding up and keeping tabs on what they're eating while for others it's a handy technique to help them get started on their calorie-controlled diet.

We generally, instinctively know what is good to eat and what we really shouldn't, but knowing a bit better exactly why can really help you shift excess weight.

Knowing how many calories you are consuming doesn't have to be a mathematical feat full of complicated equations.

There are plenty of websites offering free calorie counting apps to help you stay on track by keeping track of the amount you are consuming.

Depending on your needs, these apps can help you see where you are slipping up or motivate you to take your weight loss plan to the next level.

All you need to do is input what you have eaten and the app does the rest. Some even make helpful recommendations as to what food you should eat more or less of.

For A Smaller You Use Smaller Plates

Trick Your Brain into Thinking Less Is More

A simple change in what you eat your food from can make a massive difference to the amount you actually consume.

This tip is all about changing perceptions and tricking the brain into thinking less or even the same is substantially more.

The bigger your plates, the less your brain thinks you are eating. The simple trick then, is use smaller plates!

Psychologists have studied this strange phenomenon and have shown it to work.

The human brain is the most mysterious of all objects in the universe and using yours to trick yours will help you feel more satisfied, psychologically and physically.

Obviously, reducing your portion sizes will have extra benefits for weight loss, but even if you pack your smaller plate with the same amount as before, you may find that you're more inclined to feel fuller faster and therefore not wolf down the lot!

Coconut Oil Amazing!

This 5 Star Superfood Has Simply Stunning Effects

If you do only one thing is this whole book, this is it! When you embark on a weight loss regime one of the most powerful tactics can be swapping the oil you cook with to something tastier and far healthier for you overall.

Coconut oil has unique properties that really make it a choice to seriously consider.

No, actually, read on and you'll agree there's nothing really to think about.

Studies show that adding coconut oil to your diet will lead to a significant reduction in both BMI and waist circumference.

Read that again.

No mention of exercise or stipulation about a healthy diet. No, the people didn't up their activity levels or start counting calories; they just added coconut oil to their diet and saw their fat slowly melt.

Think then what adding a little to your new, healthier, calorie conscious diet combined with your increased activity and boosted metabolic rate can do!

Because MCTS Burn Fat

Not only can coconut oil help with appetite reduction and help fat burning it is loaded with MCTS (Medium Chain Triglycerides) - fatty acids that get metabolized in a totally different way to other fats.

Most fats are long-chain but MCTs go straight to the liver and are either used there as energy or turned into ketone bodies (which are linked to therapeutic benefits for brain disorders such as epilepsy and Alzheimer's).

Studies show boosting your levels of MCTs reduces your overall calorie intake because you just don't feel the need for more food and are less likely to experience the want for a weight loss slip-up snack.

These fats also seem to help the body burn more energy with one study suggesting it could be by as much as 5%.

It might be considered exotic in the West, but coconuts have for centuries been a dietary staple that has helped people and communities thrive with excellent health and an absence of heart disease.

It is very effective in helping you fight fat around your internal organs and abdominal cavity - the most dangerous fat associated with modern health problems and disease.

A Timely Reminder

Look Good but Also Live Better and Longer

Your motives for losing weight may be simple pure vanity and looking good - and if that works to keep you inspired, active and eating healthy, brilliant!

But it's also worth remembering that being overweight puts you at risk and is far more than a cosmetic problem.

Being overweight cannot only diminish your quality of life immensely, it can, and for far too many definitely does, reduce your life expectancy. That's why it's good to be reminded about what being overweight actually means and the real risk you put yourself at by not doing something about it.

Overweight people risk coronary heart disease, which can lead to angina, heart attacks or fatal heart failure.

High blood pressure causes damage to the body in many ways and is far more common in obese or overweight people.

So too are the chances of having a stroke and type 2 diabetes, both of which are life threatening and incredibly debilitating.

Abnormal blood fats are also more common and can lead to heart disease. Your cancer risk is higher, so too the likelihood of osteoarthritis - a common joint problem of the knees, lower back and hips that cause pain and immobility.

Sleep apnea is also a symptom with fat round the neck narrowing the airway and making it harder to breathe.

Gallstones, a cause of severe stomach and back pain are more occurring in overweight people.

Obese women can experience menstrual problems and even infertility.

Green for Go...And Put the Kettle On!

Tea to Speed Up Fat Break-Up

Scientists aren't sure how or why but they are agreed that green tea increases the speed with which the body breaks down fat.

Several studies have suggested it as a real and powerful tool to boost weight loss, but evidence published in The Journal of Nutrition credits the popular brew with fat-busting properties.

The claims are that green tea targets belly fat and so can help you make a big difference to your appearance, health and overall weight.

The precise mechanisms employed to achieve this are still being researched, and green tea is also believed to aid blood sugar regulation and improve insulin sensitivity.

This helps calm and cut cravings for refined carbs and sugar - so it will help reduce the risk of developing diabetes and have a very positive impact on your daily calorie consumption.

Swapping your daily sugary-soda for cups of green tea will, unequivocally, have an incredible, visible result on your waistline and weight.

So, go on, put the kettle on. And remember, it's tea with no sugar!

Final Words

I would like to thank you for purchasing my book and I hope I have been able to help you and educate you on something new.

If you have enjoyed this book and would like to share your positive thoughts, could you please take 30 seconds of your time to go back and give me a review on my Amazon book page.

I greatly appreciate seeing these reviews because it helps me share my hard work.

You can leave me a review on Amazon.com

Again, thank you and I wish you all the best!

Enjoying this book?

Check out my other best sellers!

Get your next book on sale here:

TopFitnessAdvice.com/go/books

Printed in Great
Britain
by Amazon